KU-428-699

Mount Everest

Nancy Dickmann

www.raintreepublishers.co.uk
Visit our website to find out
more information about
Raintree books.

To order:

☎ Phone 0845 6044371

▤ Fax +44 (0) 1865 312263

✉ Email myorders@raintreepublishers.co.uk

Customers from outside the UK please telephone +44 1865 312262

Raintree is an imprint of Capstone Global Library
Limited, a company incorporated in England and
Wales having its registered office at 7 Pilgrim
Street, London, EC4V 6LB – Registered company
number: 6695582

Text © Capstone Global Library Limited 2013
First published in hardback in 2013
The moral rights of the proprietor have
been asserted.

Edited by Rebecca Rissman, Dan Nunn, and
    Catherine Veitch
Designed by Cynthia Della-Rovere
Levelling by Jeanne Clidas
Picture research by Elizabeth Alexander
Production by Victoria Fitzgerald
Originated by Capstone Global Library
Printed and bound in China by CTPS

ISBN 978 1 406 24191 4
16 15 14 13 12
10 9 8 7 6 5 4 3 2 1

**British Library Cataloguing in Publication
Data**
Dickmann, Nancy.
Mount Everest. -- (Explorer tales)
915.4'96'04-dc22
A full catalogue record for this book is available
from the British Library.

Acknowledgements
We would like to thank the following for permission to
reproduce photographs: © Royal Geographical Society
p. 16; Alamy pp. 6 (© Image Source), 9 (© Ashley
Cooper), 10 (© Pictorial Press Ltd), 13 (© Vintage Image),
14 (© Royal Geographical Society), 19 (© Ashley Cooper
Pics); Corbis pp. 12–13 (© Stefan Chow), 15 (© Stefan
Chow), 27 (© Aurora Photos/ Peter McBride); Getty
Images pp. 8 (Jake Norton), 11 (AFP), 17 (Butch Adams/
Stone), 18 (Hulton Archive/ Keystone), 20 (Robert
Harding/ David Pickford), 26 (AFP Photo/ Namgyal
Sherpa), 29 (AFP); Nature Picture Library p. 7 (John
Downer); Press Association Images pp. 21 (AP Photo/Super
Sherpas LLC), 24 (PRESSENS BILD), 25 (BILD/PRESSENS);
Reuters p. 22; Rex Features p. 23 (c.Everett Collection);
Shutterstock p. 4 (© Ignacio Salaverria).

Cover photographs of Tenzing Norgay and Edmund Hillary
reproduced with permission of Press Association Images
(AP); map of Asia, c. 1580, reproduced with permission
of Sanders of Oxford, rare prints & maps (www.
sandersofoxford.com); Top of the World – Mount Everest
and Nuptse reproduced with permission of Shutterstock
(© Momentum). Background image of Mount
Everest reproduced with permission of Shutterstock
(© Ignacio Salaverria).

Every effort has been made to contact copyright holders
of material reproduced in this book. Any omissions will
be rectified in subsequent printings if notice is given to
the publisher.

Contents

Some words are shown in bold, **like this**. You can find out what they mean by looking in the glossary.

The top of the world

Have you ever wanted to climb a mountain? Mountains tower high above the land, and none is taller than Mount Everest. It is so high and cold that snow covers it all year round.

Mount Everest is between Nepal and China.

NEPAL

Mt Everest

Tibet

CHINA

INDIA

| 0 | 500 | 1000 miles |
| 0 | 500 | 1000 kilometres |

North
West — East
South

It is hard to breathe on Everest. At the top there is very little **oxygen** in the air. When climbers do not get enough oxygen, they get headaches, feel sick, and see things that are not really there!

DID YOU KNOW?
The only animals you might see at the top of Mount Everest are bar-headed geese. They fly over the **summit**.

Climbing Mount Everest

Climbing Mount Everest seems like a crazy idea. The cold, snow, ice, and falling rocks make it very dangerous. But, thousands of people have tried.

DID YOU KNOW?
For every 19 successful climbs, one climber has died on Mount Everest.

ice axe

Mountain climbers use tools such as ice axes and **crampons** to grip the ice.

crampon

First to the top?

One morning in 1924, George Mallory and Andrew Irvine left camp and headed for the **summit**. They were using a new tool, **oxygen** in bottles, to help them breathe. But they never came back.

oxygen bottle

George Mallory

DID YOU KNOW?

When asked why he wanted to climb Mount Everest, Mallory said, "Because it is there".

No one knows if Mallory and Irvine reached the **summit**. In 1999, Mallory's body was found lower down the mountain. The mystery is still unsolved.

DID YOU KNOW?

Mallory had a camera, which has never been found. Could it hold a photo of the summit?

Success at last

No one had got to the top of Mount Everest by 1953. On 29 May, Edmund Hillary and Tenzing Norgay were almost there. There was a 12-metre wall of rock between them and the **summit**. Was this the end of their climb?

Norgay

Hillary

DID YOU KNOW?
Today there are ropes in place to help climbers up the rock wall. It is called the Hillary Step.

Norgay stands on the **summit**.

Hillary found a **vertical** crack at the edge of the wall. He wedged himself in and pulled himself up. Then he helped Norgay. After a little more climbing, the two men were standing on top of the world!

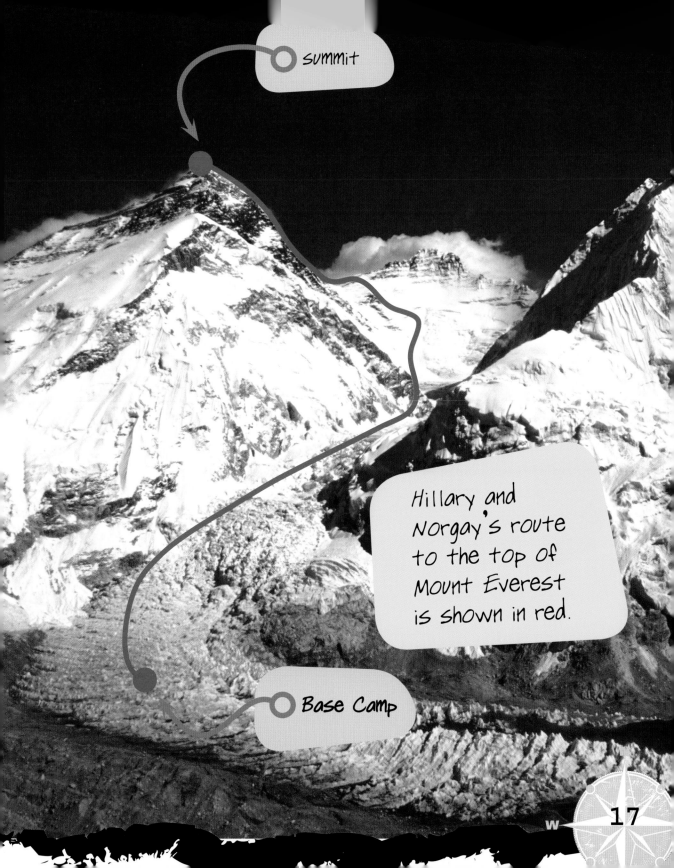

summit

Hillary and Norgay's route to the top of Mount Everest is shown in red.

Base Camp

Climbing

In 1978, Reinhold Messner and Peter Habeler climbed Mount Everest without using bottled **oxygen**. They thought that using bottled oxygen was cheating! Climbing without it meant they had to stop every few steps to catch their breath.

Messner points to the **summit** of Everest on a photograph.

goggles

DID YOU KNOW?

When sunlight bounces off snow it can cause snow blindness. Climbers wear goggles to protect their eyes.

Super Sherpas

The Sherpa people live in the area around Mount Everest. They often work as mountain guides. Many climbers are amazed at how well the Sherpas cope with **altitude**.

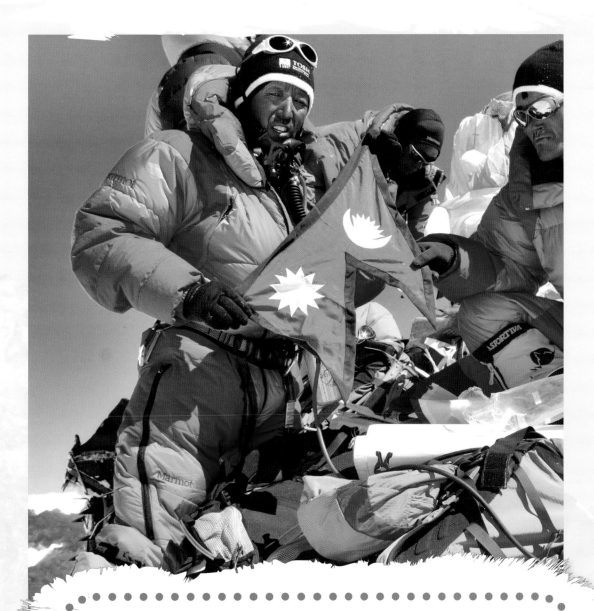

DID YOU KNOW?

Apa Sherpa holds the record for climbing Mount Everest the most times. In 2011, he climbed it for the 21st time.

Crazy descents

In 2000, Davorin Karničar skied from the **summit** back to the **Base Camp**. Climbing up had taken several days. Skiing down took just five hours! He has skied down mountains on all seven **continents**.

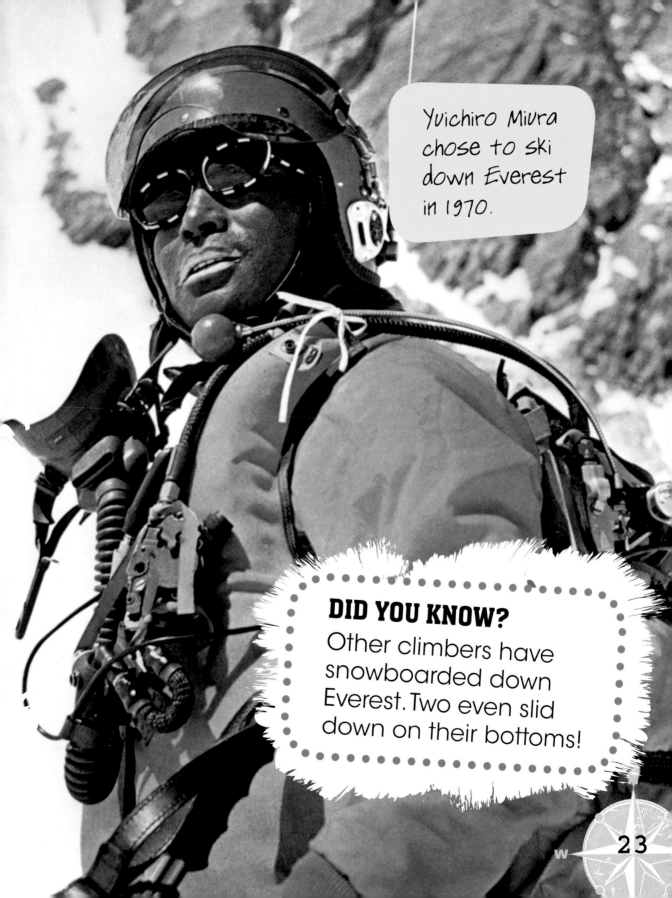

Yuichiro Miura chose to ski down Everest in 1970.

DID YOU KNOW?
Other climbers have snowboarded down Everest. Two even slid down on their bottoms!

Mount Everest by bike

Most climbers fly to Nepal. In 1996, Göran Kropp rode his bike – from Sweden! It took five months. He climbed Mount Everest alone, came down, and cycled back to Sweden.

Kropp

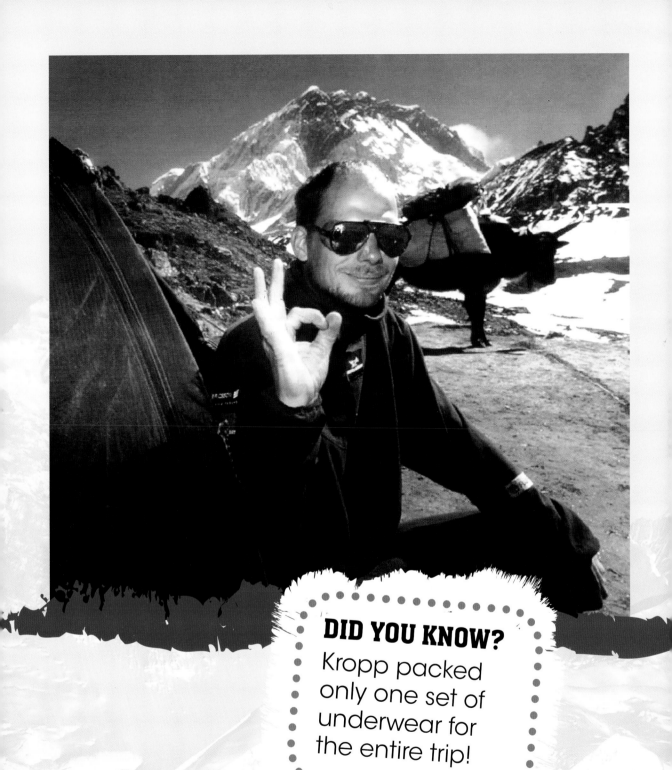

DID YOU KNOW?
Kropp packed
only one set of
underwear for
the entire trip!

Mount Everest today

Hundreds of climbers visit Mount Everest each year. That means a lot of litter. There are no bins, so what is left behind stays there – even dead bodies!

People are working to clean up Mount Everest.

Climbers spend several weeks at **Base Camp** getting used to the altitude.

Timeline

1924   George Mallory and Andrew Irvine disappear on Mount Everest.

1953   Edmund Hillary and Tenzing Norgay are the first to reach the **summit**.

1978   Reinhold Messner and Peter Habeler climb Mount Everest without bottled **oxygen**.

1980   Messner climbs Everest without oxygen again, this time by himself.

1996   Göran Kropp cycles to Mount Everest and back.

1999   Mallory's body is found near the summit.

2000   Davorin Karničar skis down Mount Everest.

2011   Apa Sherpa climbs Mount Everest for the 21st time.

Explorer's checklist

If you want to climb a mountain you will need the right gear:

climbing suit: like a duvet with arms and legs!

gloves: a thin inner pair and thick mittens to cover them

goggles: to protect your eyes from snow blindness

crampons: for gripping the ice

oxygen: for breathing – unless you think that's cheating!

ice axe: for cutting steps in snow – and gripping if you start to fall!

boots: must be light but **sturdy**, warm, and waterproof

Glossary

altitude height above sea level. It is hard to breathe at high altitude as there is very little oxygen.

Base Camp place where climbers stay before climbing Mount Everest

continent very large land mass. There are seven continents on Earth.

crampon metal plate with spikes fixed to a boot, used for climbing on ice or rock

oxygen gas in the air. We need oxygen to breathe.

sturdy strong and well-built

summit top or highest point of a mountain

vertical straight up and down

Find out more

Books

Freaky Peaks (Horrible Geography), Anita Ganeri (Scholastic, 2009)

Mountains (Habitat Survival), Melanie Waldron (Raintree, 2012)

The World's Most Amazing Mountains (Landform Top Tens), Michael Hurley (Raintree, 2010)

Websites

kids.nationalgeographic.com/kids/games/geographygames/quizyournoodle-mount-everest/
Take a quiz about Mount Everest.

kids.nationalgeographic.com/kids/stories/peopleplaces/sherpa/
Find out lots of information about Sherpas.

Index